When Pastors Pray
The Prayers and Psalms of Pastors

Collected and Edited by
Richard Leslie Parrott, Ph.D.

This volume of prayers is dedicated to the
pastors and students who are
an inspiration in my soul,
the challenge of my work, and
a great joy to my heart.

(Judas) was stopped by the sound of a familiar voice at prayer. He stood listening. Somewhere off in the deeper foliage there, where he remembered a white boulder half buried in the earth, Jesus of Nazareth was on His knees. Judas could hear the suffering voice:

"My Father! If it be possible, let this cup pass from me!"

The nostrils of Judas twisted in disdain.

"Afraid?" he murmured. "He is afraid! He is praying to be let off—to escape."

But Jesus was not done with His praying, "Nevertheless, not as I will, but as you will."

Fulton Oursler
The Greatest Story Ever Told

Forward

"Jesus went up into the mountain by himself to pray" (Matthew 14:23). Prayer has been one of the formational aspects to the faith community known as Ashland Theological Seminary. One of our core values is Spiritual Formation. This process of nurturing an intimate relationship with God leads to a deeper life of prayer.

Throughout our campus, you can witness students in prayer every day. Whether they are walking or sitting quietly in the prayer garden, meditating in our prayer room, reflecting quietly by the bronzes of "The Divine Servant" or "Fishers of Men," or praying with one another...students are in prayer.

When Pastors Pray is a collection of prayers from pastors in the Doctor of Ministry program and the Church Renewal program. Within these pages you will see the heart of pastors in an intimate relationship with God. You will sense their pain and struggles as well as their hope and celebration. You will feel their passion for God.

We wanted to make this book available to the special friends of Ashland Theological Seminary as a way of saying thank you for your prayers on our behalf. We hope the prayers within will touch your prayer life as they reinforce our desire to seek God.

Dr. Frederick J. Finks, President
Ashland Theological Seminary
July 4, 2002

Contents

When the Pastor's Spouse Prays

When Pastors Pray:
Introduction

Pastors are viewed, and rightly so, as men and women who bring "a word from the Lord" to the congregation. They share the message from God to God's people.

Yet, speaking "from the Lord" is only half the conversation. Pastors also speak to the Lord out of the love, joy, fear, confusion, and sadness found in the congregation. These emotions of the people are carried in the heart of the pastor and brought to God, often as the pastor's personal pleading.

This is a book that reports what pastors say to God in the privacy of this deeply intimate conversation. When pastors pray "from the depths" (Psalm 130), it is honest and vulnerable, intense and sometimes shocking, yet filled with the Spirit.

The prayers in this book were not written for the pulpit, but are expressions of private spiritual encounters of blessing or lament or vengeance or thanksgiving. Each is a small container of the reality of a committed spiritual life. They reflect the prayers of the Psalms and the prayers of Jesus.

If you read carefully, you will hear the echo of your own pastor's heart. You will also hear the heart of the Chief Shepherd (1 Peter 5:4) of us all.

Why read private prayers?

There is a long and worthy tradition in Christian spirituality of reading personal prayers. The Book of Psalms is the biblical foundation of this practice. The Book of Psalms teach us how to speak back to God. And, the lesson of The Psalms is clear: God desires honest speech. There is no such thing as "biting your lip" or "censoring your prayer" in The Psalms.

Reading and reflecting on private prayers, including the private prayers of pastors, is a spiritual exercise that can cultivate your own honest conversation with God. These prayers:

- Will give you greater understanding and empathy with the heart of pastors.

- Will provide a guide to deep, honest, and secret prayer.

- Will turn your heart to deeper devotion and your soul on a search of scripture.

- Will give you courage to express "from the depths" in the presence of your loving God.

How to read private prayers?

In reading the private prayers of pastors, there are a few spiritual rules that will guide you to greater depth in your own prayers:

1. **Don't analyze or judge**. In our world, the media provide instant analysis and survey results on almost every word uttered by our national leaders. This pattern of judgment may be needed in the public arena, but will quench the Spirit in the realm of the soul. Rather than an attitude of evaluation, approach these prayers with a spirit of identification. Ask, *"what, in this prayer, speaks the truth of my soul?"*

2. **Be Open and Honest**. Often, our "spiritual conversations" with others are filled with hiding and dodging the truth of our inner lives. Read these prayers with a dedication to the truth. What is the truth in your feelings, your thinking, and your attitude? Be it blessings or cursings, let them be discovered and expressed before God. Ask, *"what do I need to say to God about the truth in my soul?"*

3. **Allow the Holy Spirit to Guide you.** There is an experience of truth shared by people of spiritual depth: When you reach the end of your words, the word of the Spirit moves in you. "We do not know what we ought to pray, but the Spirit himself intercedes for us with groans that words cannot express" (Romans 8:26). Ask, *"Holy Spirit, what do you want to say for me and in me?"*

4. **Search the Scriptures with your Soul**. We have been taught to search the scriptures with our minds. This is good and proper. But, in the depth of the soul's struggle or

delight, the mind can only point in the right direction. The soul must take the adventure, must explore spiritual and personal terrain. The soul does not seek so much to understand God as to experience God, to encounter God afresh. Ask, *"God, I need you; come to my soul."*

This little volume is collected from five years of working with students in the Doctor of Ministry program, and three years of working with pastors in the Church Renewal program. These prayers are their courageous gifts to you. As I read the words of these women and men of God, the depth of their pain and blessing moves my soul to deeper confession, conviction, and consecration.

Richard Leslie Parrott
June 2002, Cape Cod

"...while it was still dark, Jesus got up, left the house and went off to a solitary place, where he prayed."
(Mark 1:35)

The Contributors

The pastor's and spouses who contributed to this book include:

John Allison

Scott Carmer

Janet Brigham
Richard Bott
Richard Boyer
Marvin Brown
Tim Burden
Clarissa Burgess
John Burgess

Kitt Kurtz Chmura
David Cooksey

Jack Davis
William Dobbs
Agoston Dobos
Jim Donnally

Greg Gilson
Cecelia Green-Barr

Larita Hand
Ulysses O. Hollowell, Jr.
G. Emery Hurd

Bryan G. Karchner
Linda Karchner

Jeff Loach

Michael Mack
Rick McCartney
Ellen Morris
Richard W. Morris

Curt Neis

DeAnn Oburn
Gene Oburn

Kristen Patt

Earl Simpson
Don Snell

Richard Taylor

Ed Utz

Richard Wallace

And, other pastors and spouses who remain
anonymous.

When Pastors Pray

In Church!?

Lord, I am tempted to leave my paper empty
  because there seems to be not enough paper or ink
  to be able to write down all my feelings.

I'm also afraid that if I do start to write,
  the tears will boot out any thoughts.

God, all I have ever wanted to do is serve You.
But nothing seemed to work out,
  not family, not money, nothing.
I never thought it would be easy
  but I never guessed that You would have allowed
  the evil in our world to come in so thoroughly and
  consume.

How can You continue to allow those
  who do evil against Your people to flourish and
  prosper <u>in church</u>!?

Many wander in malice and wound the innocent,
  yet, are never called to account in this life.

I feel completely broken inside,
  used, abused, and a failure.
We saw the evil and felt utterly
  powerless to stop it.

Where were You, and where are You now!?
I AM ANGRY!!!
I'm so angry I can't even begin to write it down.
So, I just cry, and pray
   that in the emotion of these tears
You feel all the pain that is bottled up in me.
I can't get out in any other way.

God, do You not see how these Pharisees
   continue their hunt for sport and personal prestige?

Don't You care?
Sheep (*Your sheep*) are being led to the slaughter.
I know all the "right" things to say
   even to myself as I write these words.
But deep down I'm afraid I might have
   lost my faith

        in You

            and the Truth,

                and Justice,

Have I lost my concern for Your people, also?

But I know that throughout Your history
            with Your people,
others have felt this way, also,
            and still You are there.

I must trust that You will
    in Your time
        deal with the things
            that are not of You.

Please make it soon!

All day long they surrounded me like a flood;
* they have completely engulfed me.*
You have taken my companions and
*   loved ones from me;*
* the darkness is my closest friend.*
*   (Psalm 88:17-18)*

Guide Me as I
Guide Your People

O Lord, I seek your face this day,
    as I have for so many days before;
to guide me as I guide your people
    to walk with me as I walk with them.

My memory of your people spans the generations,
    mothers and fathers, sons and daughters,
stories and tragedies, rejoicing and mourning,
    all carried within the memory of your servant.

O Lord, I seek your face this day,
    as I have for so many days before;
to guide me as I guide your people
    to walk with me as I walk with them.

My work with your people spans the years,
    preaching and teaching, loving and caring,
buildings and meetings, committees and teas,
    carried within the mind of your servant.

O Lord, I seek your face this day,
    as I have for so many days before;
to guide me as I guide your people
    to walk with me as I walk with them.

My love for your people spans the days,
    birthdays, weddings, dedications and funerals,
tears and laughter, gifts and friendship
    carried within the heart of your servant.

O Lord, I seek your face this day,
    as I have for so many days before;
to guide me as I guide your people
    to walk with me as I walk with them.

My hope for your people spans the future
    growth and vitality, maturity and service,
pastors and missionaries, evangelists and musicians
    carried in the soul of your servant.

My time with your people spans this day
    calls and visits, sermons and lessons,
a ministry of years, yet a ministry of moments
    carried in the call of your servant

O Lord, I seek your face this day,
    as I have for so many days before;
to guide me as I guide your people
    to walk with me as I walk with them.

I have fought the good fight, I have finished the race, I have kept the faith. Now there is in store for me the crown of righteousness, which the Lord, the righteous Judge, will award to me on that day – and not only to me, but also to all who have longed for his appearing.
(2 Timothy 3:7-8)

Blessing

O God, You are the loving, personal God of my life.
You, Holy Father, are the source of my strength,
the encourager who always listens to the
      complaints of my struggling heart.
You have called me and confirmed
      Your call through Your Presence.

You continue to be the constant, steady,
      A Presence in a time of transition.
I praise You, Father, because of Your faithfulness,
friendship, and words of encouragement.

Praise the Lord, O my soul;
  All my inmost being, praise his holy name.
Praise the Lord, O my soul;
  And forget not all his benefits.
      (Psalm 103:1-2)

Is This What You Had in Mind

O God,
        The whole thing crumbled
and slipped through my fingers.
        Is this what You had in mind?

I don't care about their criticisms or accusations –
        They acted like twits.
        So did I.
But...to crumble, fall apart.
        Is this what You had in mind?

Can't You see how
        Satan loves and the world mocks –
They mock me not; they mock You!
        Is this what You had in mind?

Come now, Lord, strengthen me now.
        Pick up the pieces.
Come now, Lord, build on them.
        Is this what You had in mind?

O my God, You are a mystery to me;
        You called me out of 1000 better choices.
Out of 10,000 better choices,
        You, O God, my God called me!

When I thought You were mistaken,
    You lifted me.
You protected me and supported me,
    and now somehow I sense
        You were right all along.

*Then I heard the voice of the Lord saying, "Whom
shall I send? And who will go for us?" And I said,
"Here am I, send me."*
                       (Isaiah 6:8)

Here I Come Again

Well, Lord, here I come again.
I have asked You to heal my wife's wrist,
       You haven't;
I asked You to heal her ears.
       I thought You had,
  but the problem is coming back again.
                        Why?

I asked a few people to do a simple thing
       like fill out some papers
  and send them in a self-addressed stamped
envelope
       and not all of them have.
Why didn't You prompt them to do that?

I am discouraged and angry.

What is my part in all this?
Where do I go from here?

He heals the broken hearted
and binds up their wounds.
        (Psalm 147:3)

This Bites

All right, God, here it is:
                                This bites.

I have done my best to serve You
  from the bottom of my heart for 25 years;
I have given up dreams of fun and ease;
sacrificed security;
  gotten the stuffing kicked out of me;
  spent years for the sake of others.

But this doesn't seem worth it.
Other times, it has. Not now.
I wish so much that some would "get it."
And the junk, Lord, the garbage that
  has been done "in Your name."
It's sickening. I am sick
  and You couldn't still be there,
  and yet I look ahead to a grueling
  doctoral program. It's not fair!
When does the joy start?
Won't it be too late for my kids?
Won't You please do some revival of Your own?
  (Just not me, of course.)
I know You've got a plan.
  I will trust.
I'd love a straight line,
  but I will wait for You.

"Meaningless, meaningless!" says the Teacher.
"Utterly meaningless! Everything is meaningless!"
            (Ecclesiastes 1:2)

You are a Rock

O God, You are a Rock!
Your Word is spoken and it is true.
Your Word is written and it is powerful.
Your Word is living and He is Lord.
Thank you for Your Word.

Your Love, O Lord, reaches deep into me.
It cradles me in the deep,
and carries me to the mountain peaks.
Your love sustains me, maintains me, and is my life.
Thank you for Your love.

Your world is quiet and still;
grass grows, earth decays,
the roses offer their perfume.
Your world is resounding –
water roars, thunder booms,
waves pound, beasts cry out.
Your world is more than I can understand;
it reflects the mystery of its Creator.
Thank you for Your world.

O God, my family is a joy.
Thank you for their smiles.
Thank you for their love.
Thank you for my family.

O God, You are my Rock.
Thank you for the wife You have given me.
She is my gift when my resources fail.
She is my reflection when I need a clear view.
She is my faith when I am in doubt.
She is Your love when I am need it.
Thank you, God, for the wife You have given me.

O God, You are my Rock.
You have not failed; You shall not.
All my days, I will serve You.
Keep my feet steady,
O God, my Rock!

*Therefore everyone who hears these words of mine
and puts them into practice is like a wise man who
built his house on the rock. The rain came down,
the streams rose, and the winds blew and beat
against that house; yet it did not fall, because it had
its foundation on the rock.*
(Matthew 7:24-25)

Your Vision of
Who I am to Become

Lord, I feel like there is not a stable or safe place
   with me now;
but the one stable place is knowing
   that You are stable.

You are the Rock on which I stand
   and often feel as if I'm slipping off.
But deep within, I know You would never
   let me fall to my death; but to my salvation.
You have inscribed me in the palm of Your hand
   from the foundation of the world and
continue to mold me into a beautiful
   work of art.

I praise You for Your vision of who I am to
   become, the lessons You have brought me,
   through laughter and pain,
And that as awesome as You have made
   the beauty of this world,
the squirrel that blends with the tree,
the colors of the grass, sky, trees.
Your greatest beauty is in the transformation
   of me into Your likeness.

May I bow to serve You
   as You have bowed to serve me.

As a mother comforts her child,
so will I comfort you;
and you will be comforted over Jerusalem."
                    (Isaiah 66:13)

My Joy

O God, You are my Joy.
You have been my guide
  as You continue to show Your love.

I praise You
  for all the love
You have shown me and all others
  who love You
  and follow You.

For the Lord your God will bless you in all your
harvest and in all the work of your hands, and your
joy will be complete.
                          (Deuteronomy 16:15b)

I have told you this so that my joy may be in you
and that your joy may be complete.
                          (John 15:11)

You Can be Trusted

Lord, we give You praise
  for You can be trusted.
Praise you for bringing us a baby,
  when the womb was closed.
Praise you for birthing a new work
  from the rubble of
hatred, discontent, and three different agendas.

Our physical baby is healthy.
Our spiritual baby is becoming healthy.
I praise You for bringing
      light from darkness,
      truth from lies.
You are good.
      You are great.
           You can be trusted.
              You are in control!

Trust in the Lord with all your heart
  and lean not on your own understanding;
in all your ways acknowledge him,
  and he will make your paths straight.
        (Proverbs 3:5-6)

Leave These People I Love?

God,
>> why does this separation
>> have to be so painful?
> Why must tears be shed
>> and ties be broken?
> I love these people,
>> and yet You are telling me to leave.
> I know there are good reasons
>> and it is in Your will
>> and You have some purpose
>>> but it hurts.

Why have You created us to feel pain?
>> How can You be still and let this happen?
> Surely You would want to comfort those You love.
>> You don't want us to suffer,
>>> do You?

Lord, at least promise You will be with me
>> through this time.
> Don't be far away in my time of need.
> If you are beside me,
>> I know I will make it.
> If You will hold my hand,
>> I will learn to depend on You.

Lord, I don't understand this place I am in.
>> You brought healing,
>> but it didn't last.

Was I unfaithful?

Did I displease You?

Was it a mean trick?

You gave me a glimpse
of what it is to be whole.

Now I commit you to God and to the word of his
grace, which can build you up and give you an
inheritance among all those who are sanctified.
(Acts 20:32)

Is This Your Punishment?

God, let me tell You what is happening in me…
I feel that this is Your punishment,
       because we were wrong.

I admit that we were wrong,
       I too.

I was not strong enough to be patient,
       to be peaceful.
I was not strong and wise enough to carry out the
       decision I felt was according to Your will.

How could we be so ungrateful?
       How could we be so merciless?
              How could I deny Your way?
Are You punishing us also for the past thoughts?

Lord, You see that I am uncertain.
I cannot see whether I was unloving,
       or that was the right thing to do?

I repent
       but I am not sure whether I should repent.
But then I do not understand why this loss
       happened to us.

Let Your will be done, not ours.
I dedicate myself and my family
And the child we hope for
       to You
              again.

Then I acknowledged my sin to you
  and did not cover up my iniquity. I said, "I will
confess my transgressions to the Lord" –
and you forgave
  the guilt of my sin.
                (Psalm 32:5)

I Hurt Deep Down

God I hurt deep down.
God I'm frustrated more of the time than not.

I feel like I fail You so many times!

You've placed Your trust in me
      and I feel like I'm failing.
You've given me a challenge
      and unless You step in;
        I can't do it!

God if I'm not able to finish this challenge,
what praise will You receive from it?

I remember how You brought us out of "there"
      when we were devastated in spirit.
I know That if You can do that
      then You can lead me now.

Oh help to fulfill the challenge.
      I will praise You!
          I will put my trust in You!

God, why did You wait twenty years to give me a
      Pastor Appreciation Day?
Didn't I do anything before that was appreciated?

Do I have Your approval?

How great is the love the Father has lavished on us,
that we should be called children of God! And that
is what we really are.
              (1 John 3:1)

One of the Hardest
Moments of Ministry

God, You are the rock for which my feet search.
You have always provided a firm foothold at the
      crucial moment.
You continue to provide the secure stepping place
      in the way You desire me to go.
I praise You for Your solid,
      Your continuous firm foundation.

God, I don't even know where to begin so I will
      start in the present.
I have tried to do what I thought You wanted
      – face the real issues of my church.
      I formed the thoughts,
      articulated the problem,
      formed the questions and began,
          for the first time,
          to embrace the problem.

Well God, You know what happened next,
So-and-so got their hands on the issue
      and accusations were made,
      and people resigned,
      and I was falsely accused
      and judged.
This was on the of the hardest moments of ministry.

This was terrible, God. If You don't restore justice,
      then how can I continue?

How will this be viewed, God,
      if You don't come
      and straighten things out?

Not only is my
      integrity at risk,
           so is Yours.

Maybe, God,
      You needed to do this to show me
      where I really am in my relationships.
      How else could the issue be
          brought to my attention?

Father, thanks for helping me to know my heart.
      I praise Your Name.
I praise You for renewed assurance of
      Your presence

In me; I see a new maturity,
         therefore
      I praise Your providence.

Free me from the trap that is set for me,
 for You are my refuge.
Into your hands I commit my spirit;
 Redeem me, O Lord, the God of truth.
         (Psalm 31:4-5)

The Darkest Night
I've Ever Seen

The road ahead leads into the darkness,
     the darkest night I've ever seen.
I can only see as far as my headlights.
     Uncertainty, fear,
          a shift in my foundation.
              What lies ahead?

Oh God, Why?
     Why did everything have to change?
        I was happy the way it was.

And now the future is uncertain.
     Angry men yell at me,
     because of
     the sin of another.

Oh God, Why?
     Why do I have
     to suffer
     because of
     another man's sin?

Why do I get letters
     of hurt and anger at my address?
God, I didn't cause this!
     Why do *I* have to live it!
     It isn't fair!

And I look and see Your dear people,
     shaken in faith, looking for help.
And You call my name.

O God! Don't You know…
      I am a weak man.
      A man with many insecurities.
      Who am I?

I am but a young man.
        Surely there is someone else.
           Someone with experience and age.
           With all this task demands.

Yet You call me.
      Oh God, it's hard.
      It is more than I can bear.

The pain is too great,

                         I should die.

Yet, from the ashes there is hope.
      A strength that is not from me.
      It is He: The Resurrected One.
      With healing in His wings.

"You can't, but I can," He says.
      And now
           I walk with Him.
      And now
           we will do it together.

Praise you Lord,
Praise You!

Hear me, O God, as I voice my complaint;
protect my life from the threat of the enemy.
                (Psalm 64:1)

Help Me in My Hour of Need

O Lord, hear my prayer.

Open Your ears to the requests of my lips.
For it is You only, Lord,
        who knows and understands me
        and can offer Hope in the face of fear.

I can hear You say,
        "This is just another chapter in your life's
        story. You look at the world with
        uncertainly, with hesitancy, and with
        caution. Why are you so afraid?"

Yes, Lord, it is the life story of me,
        afraid again to take a new step,
        to leave the past and live in the present.
The chapter just behind me had its share of grief;
        it did not easily flow.
Yet the one that lies before me with its unknown
        blank pages seems to be my foe.

Can I trust in You, Lord,
        in this hour of change and upheaval?
How can I know You won't leave me
        to do everything on my own?
I want to stay behind the door, to shut out the world,
        and to gaze upon the familiar
        furnishings of my past life
        in that land by the sea.

You call me to step forth and seize the day,
        to immerse myself in Your presence,
        to study the Word,
        and to learn to live in freedom from the
        structured system of the past.

Lord, why did You choose me?
What about others that are younger and smarter?
What talents or gifts do I possess that
        You seem so eager to use?

Did I displease You as priest?
Was I so ill-fit or inflexible for my task that
You felt it imperative to uproot me
        and transplant me to the desert?

I do not know how things will get done here.
Do You know that feeling, Lord?
Can You understand what I'm going through?

At night my pillow absorbs the wetness of my tears,
which flow from my heart full of fear and anxiety.

Help me in my hour of need,
        O God of all compassion.
Give me courage and faith that conquers fear.
Give me feet to take the steps.

A voice of one calling;
  "In the desert prepare
  the way for the Lord";
make straight in the wilderness
a highway for our God.
                    (Isaiah 40:3)

My Feelings are Running Away

Oh Lord, I feel I have lost control.
My feelings are running away, dragging me behind.

I got worked up yesterday
             and today,
                    I'm burning!
Burning with fiery passion.
Maybe some of it good,
        maybe some of it bad.

My anger is burning hotter and hotter
        like the desert sun.
I do not know with whom or with
        what I am so angry.

Lord, forgive me in Your mercy,
        but some of the indignation
may be toward You.

How long will You allow Your so-called people
        to thumb their noses
            at You
                and Your Word?

How long will You permit Your messenger
        to see and hear
        "no results of this ministry"
in Your Holy Name?

Lord, I know I am angry with these people,
        but Lord,
            it's not without cause!

I am angry with myself
for letting myself get into this situation.
        O Lord!
                Deliver me now.

Pour Your cool refreshing waters
        into the fires of my soul.
Purify any sin from the anger, that my indignation
may be just and righteous only.

Vindicate Your servant in the
        Servant of servants Himself.
Help me, O God!

Help me now!

Search me, O God, and know my heart;
  Test me and know my anxious thoughts.
See if there is any offensive way in me,
  And lead me in the way everlasting.
                        (Psalm 139:23-24)

I Am Their Sister

Lord, I am angry with the way Your children
       are handling Your church,
You told me to be angry but to sin not,
       but the rage inside of me
       will cause me to sin with my mouth,
I will say things I should not say
       about the Leaders
             You have called and ordained
       to serve Your house.

They say with their mouths
       that they *"love God our Father
       and Jesus Christ our Lord,"*

but I am their sister
       and they treat me as though I am
                not part of
                    You.

In my distress, I call unto You, Lord,
       because I know in my flesh,
I will make the wrong decisions
       concerning Your children.

Help me, Lord, to hear
Your still voice in this matter.

*The tongue has the power of life and death,
And those who love it will eat its fruit.*
              (Proverbs 18:21)

I Try

Lord,
   why do those who will not receive me
     claim that I do not listen?
They make presumptions on my leadership ability
   without letting me love them.
            I try.

But every time I reach out in love,
   my hand is bitten.
The pain in my bitten hand is too easily
   transferred into my heart
     where hardness forms.

It is that hardness that angers me –
   perhaps more
   than the antagonists themselves.

Part of me wants to beg for mercy –
   on my part and theirs –
while another part screams at You
   to do justice
     and kick those detractors out.

But You are rich in mercy and love
   and I can only pray to share what measure
   You have given me.

Out of the depths I cry to you, O Lord;
O Lord, hear my voice.
       (Psalm 130:1)

A Young Man Died Today

From the mountain downward I plunged into the
depth of my angry soul.

Today a beautiful young man had to die.

Was it fate, God? Can You tell me?
I would really like to know!

He too was Your child. Your creation. Like me.
Like everybody! God! Where were You?

And where were You the day that he bombed the
life out of all those precious people?
Remember the dear blessed souls
that You miraculously created?

Men! Women! Children!

And why could he not hear You screaming?

Timothy! No, don't do it!

You were screaming,
        weren't You?
                Please tell me You were.

Please answer, God!   Why was he left alone?
Alone on a path to destruction.

Why did You not show him the love he needed
to bring his heart alive with compassion?

Was there no one who could reach him?
Were there no gentle hands
        to hold him
                when he cried?

Did You hear him crying, God?

And, God, I have another question for You:
How can I ever believe in Your omnipotence,
                        Your omniscience?

Men, women, children, little babies, God!
Innocent, gentle, loving people –
blown into tiny little pieces –
How could this happen?

I am angry, God.
Who is out there stealing away Your greatness?
        Can evil really outwit You?
                It would seem so!

A beautiful young man died today.
        Executed!
                Why did evil win?

It snatched up his heart and soul.
It exploited him. Twisted him. Abandoned him.

And where were You? Dear God, where were You?
                        I need to know!

52

Are You there, God!?
I love You!
I believe in You.

But angry "whys?" are spilling
into my spirit
and my soul.

I am very sad.

Please, God,
comfort us all!

And, God, let me comfort You too.

I remember my affliction and my wandering,
the bitterness and the gall.
I well remember them,
and my soul is downcast within me.
Yet this I call to mind
And therefore I have hope:

Because of the Lord's great love we are not
consumed, for his compassions never fail.
They are new every morning;
Great is your faithfulness.
(Lamentations 3:19-23)

Fear & Faith

Of what should I be afraid?
The Lord is near me.
Yet there are times when I feel overwhelmed
by the reality of what is.
I know what God says, but yet there are times
when I hesitate.
The Lord says go, and I say wait.

It is at these times when fear challenges faith.
Fear is often birthed by the challenge to move
between two spheres,
From the known to the unknown.
Faith is ready to make such a move,
but fear says wait.

I thank the Lord that I am learning to deal with fear,
not through my eyes, but the eyes of faith.
I must relay on the strength of the Lord;
as He says go in His strength,
I can say yes.

*"...And surely I will be with you always, to the very
end of the age."*
(Matthew 28:20)

Thorn in the Flesh

Lord, You have always been gracious
    beyond measure;
You have given me far more than I deserve.
You have brought me to this place to serve
    these people;
You have led me to this hour for Your work.

I have tried to be faithful, though I am still growing;
I have embraced discipleship in spite of my sin.
I depend upon Your grace to do my duty here;
I need Your help to shepherd this flock.

Deliver me from a staff of assistants
    who love self more than work.
Who work not for You but for money and for ego.
They willingly tear down
    in order to build themselves up.
They destroy the team for the sake of one.

They have become a thorn in my flesh, Lord.
They bring pain to the joy of this task.

I want them gone from this place;
Their continued presence is agony for me.

If the afflicting presence of
    these assistants on this staff
        is meant to help me grow,

please show me how they will help me mature as a
    pastor.
If they are from the Evil One,
    deliver me from testing and temptation.

Help me to sing Your praises in the midst of trial;
    lift my eyes beyond the pain of this moment.
Bring me to the place where I can love my enemies;
    make me see them as Your children too.

I will love You in them, O Lord;
    grant me a willing heart.

*To keep me from becoming conceited because of
these surpassingly great revelations, there was
given me a thorn in my flesh, a messenger of Satan,
to torment me. Three times I pleaded with the Lord
to take it away from me. But he said to me, "My
grace is sufficient for you, for my power is made
perfect in weakness." Therefore I will boast all the
more gladly about my weaknesses, so that Christ's
power may rest in me.*

(2 Corinthians 12:7-9)

For the Love
Of My Children

Lord, the terror is in my stomach;
     the fear is in my soul.
My mind is numb,
     and I don't know what to do.

How can I be a father
     when I am not with them every day?
How can I guide them
     when all I have is the phone?

She can take them from me,
     and the system will not support me.
The kids hear only her,
     and I have a voice with no sound.

But my love for You is great;
     my trust in You undaunted.
They will know their father,
     and I will know my children.

My trust is in the Lord;
His love will be in them.
I know His love, and it is faithful.
They know His love, and it is faithful.

I know their love,
        and they know mine;
        our relationship is strong.

And He will keep it safe.

As a father has compassion on his children,
  So the Lord has compassion on those who fear
him.
                (Psalm 103:13)

More Than I Can Do God

Yes, I **am** angry...and why not?
You've surrounded me with people who see
      only their desires –
      they believe their desires are the same as
         everyone around them.

You've Called me to a place where they don't
      understand that
      Ministry is more than "being with people,"
      Ministry is more than "visitation,"
      Ministry is more than...
         more than I can do, God.

...more than I can do, God!
At least, I can't do it right now, and not by myself...
         that's how I'm feeling today.
It feels like You've left me
      to try and help them to be Your people,
      and then You've gone off
         to attend other matters.
         to more important matters.

Well, Great and Divine, All-Knowing One...
         a crisis is brewing *here*.
      A storm that is going to have dire results
         is on the horizon,
         is moving toward us,
         is threatening to overwhelm.

LISTEN TO ME...please.
I need Your shelter.
I need Your guidance.
I need You

Help me to find You as my Source, again,
so I can be
re-filled...
re-freshed...
re-framed...
ready to minister to Your people, again.

Help me to tone down the arrogance in my heart,
so I can really hear what You're saying
through them.

And maybe...just a bit...would You open their ears,
to hear what You're saying
through me?

Even in my anger...even in my frustration and fear...
I know You're here,
loving them...
loving me.

Selah. Amen. So be it.

But you are a shield around me, O Lord,
  My Glorious One, who lifts up by head.
To the Lord I cry aloud,
  And he answers me from his holy hill.
                              (Psalm 3:3-4)

I Don't Understand

God, may I tell You what is happening in me?
I want You to know, people are misunderstanding
    my intentions,
    my reasoning,
    what I believe You told me to do.

You told me, or at least allowed me
    to accept the call that I have.
I believe this to be true and right and good;
    then why all the confusion
        on the part of a few?

Father, do You not understand the hurt
    that I and others have had to face
        because of certain people?
Have You not seen the hurt
    my wife has had to go through lately?
Have You not seen the un-sureness
    that my children are feeling?

You brought me here to face a lot of *"schmut."*
I could have stayed where I was and had it better.
    A least I knew my enemies
        and where I stood.

I appeal for Your righteousness, Your justice,
    Your mercy and love to right the wrongs.

I appeal to Your glory; that unless You act,
    Satan will be seen to be the victor.

All the works of righteousness
        that have gone before
        will be remembered no more
        in light of this horrible chaos.
I appeal my case and cause to Your loving holiness.

Father, I am learning to just stand
        when everything else around
                me is falling apart.
I am learning that
        when I cannot,
                You have just begun.
I am learning that in spite of the pain and suffering,
        if I will look for You, towards You,
        I will see You and will be found by You.

Truly, when it's all said and done,
        what really counts is
        to just allow You
        to do Your work
                in and through me.
                "Not my will but Yours be done!"

*Blessed are you when people insult you, persecute
you and falsely say all kinds of evil against you
because of me. Rejoice and be glad, because great
is your reward in heaven, for in the same way they
persecuted the prophets who were before you.*
                (Matthew 5:11-12)

The Lord of Life Reigns!

The Lord of Life reigns!
He produces the fruit upon the plains,
and says to the fish of the lakes,
"Multiply!"
The hills sing the praises
of His Holy Name.
And the people
Yes, His children see His wonders
And are glad.
Come, my soul, sing His praises.
Declare His glory in all the land.
The Lord of Life reigns!

The earth is the Lord's, and everything in it,
the world, and all who live in it;
for he founded it upon the seas
and established it upon the waters.
(Psalm 24:1-2)

What Will Become of Me?

My Lord and my God, what will become of me?
Day by day I am aging.
My energy and strength diminish.
My memory fails me time and time again.
When I am traveling down the road,
I cannot remember where I am,
or where I was going.
I cry out to You, "Help me, Lord!"
What will become of me?
I am useless and spent.

The circumstances of my life change
like tumultuous whitewater.
I cannot stay the course.
The unnerving changes leave me
spinning and reeling.
I am lost in frightening confusion.
Security and comfort elude me.

My daughters and sons are leaving me.
They have no need of me anymore.
I have become old and useless, like a worn-out rag.
I have become like a common fixture of no interest.
I am lost in a deep lonely darkness.
I turn to You, but You are too far away.
What will become of me?
I don't know where to turn.

I am afraid of the endless trials and confusion.
I am afraid of the unending loneliness and despair.
I am afraid of the ceaseless darkness and emptiness.
Where is my help? There is none.
I wander alone and afraid. How long, O Lord?

The deep and terrifying darkness surrounds me.
Can You hear me, Lord?
I cannot find my way in this darkness.
I cannot find my way in this confusion.
I don't know where to turn.
I have lost all comfort and security.
I am alone and abandoned.
I have no one to help me.

Death is waiting for me behind the door.
I have lost my redemption.
I walk in the valley of the shadow of death.
You are not there with crook or staff.
I stand in the assembly of Your people,
and they know that I am no one.
They know that I am nothing.
The people see my worthlessness.
Surely they will stone me; I stand alone trembling,
waiting for the stoning to begin.

I stand alone in the vast assembly
of my jeering adversaries.
The lions are circling; their roaring is
fierce and deafening.
My enemies cheer at my demise.
I am alone without help.
Death is my only company.

Closer the lions come;
they charge me now with wide-open jaws,
with razor-sharp teeth ready to tear at my flesh.
My enemies rise to their feet and cheer louder.
I close my eyes awaiting the pain and death.
I am paralyzed with fear.
I want to cry out, but no sound comes forth.

I want to run, but my legs tremble;
I stumble and fall.
I have no escape.
The Deep Darkness of Death devours me.
Only You, O Lord, can rescue me.
Save me, Lord. Hear my cries.

My God, my God, why have you forsaken me...
Roaring lions tearing their prey
  Open their mouths wide against me.
I am poured out like water,
  And all my bones are out of joint.
My heart has turned to wax;
  It has melted away within me.
                    (Psalm 22:1, 13-14)

Is This My Fault?

I need you to listen to me, Lord,
>because sometimes it seems as though
>You are the only one with an attentive spirit.

You are the one,
>the Scriptures say, who casts out fear.

You are the one,
>the Church says, who can always be trusted.

You are the one,
>my friends say, who will always save me.

You are the one,
>so says my heart, who really knows.

I have been set upon by forces
>which I cannot name and cannot control.

Are they demons,
>or are they bad decisions?

Are they supernatural,
>or are they simply a result of my inability or
>unwillingness to take control of my life?

Whatever they are, they haunt me.

Unless you have experienced it,
>don't try to tell me just to buck up and
>cast my cares aside.

There are so many out there for whom depression is
>simply a word in the dictionary.

They don't know
      the darkness and the depth of despair.

They don't know
      what it means to be in a hole and unable to
      find the footholds to climb out.

They don't know
      the loneliness and
            the fear and
                  the unknowing.

            Is this my fault?
Have I responded stupidly to life's circumstances?
      Or, it is simply brain chemistry gone awry?

It is sort of a "Catch 22," this depression.
I need to get the juices flowing again,
      get active again,
      get a new perspective,
      catch a glimpse of the possibilities,
      expect miracles to happen.

But you need the energy to do that and
      depression saps your strength,
      destroys your confidence, and
      convinces you that
            this is as
                  good as
                        it gets.

What else can I do but trust God to
       walk with me through this deep valley?

What else can I do but expect God to
       keep me at all times,
       even during the dark

                              night of my soul?

Hear me, O God, as I voice my complaint;
Protect my life from the threat of the enemy.
(Psalm 64:1)

69

Stand Up!

Lord of all, I feel so small
>when those giants stand up in their ranks,
>and my knees actually begin to shake,
>and every cell in my body screams, "Run!"

My will wants to avoid any confrontation.
>Where will the courage come from?

Now it's dark, completely dark.
>And, in the dark are many things.
>I can feel them, sense them, bump into them.
But I cannot avoid them in the dark, or I would.
The dark has closed in on me and I feel choked.

Lord, how I praise You that You see clearly
>in the dark,
That You know all that's in the dark
>and have already defeated them.
Thank you that I am not alone in this dark, ever.

Lord, how I praise You that when the giant stands,
>he is small when You stand.
>Stand up, O Lord, with me;
>>stand up in me.

Moses answered the people, "Do not be afraid.
Stand firm and you will see the deliverance the Lord
will bring you today.
>>*(Exodus 14:13)*

What If?

What will happen –
When the medical bills come
And, the claim is denied
And I have to get another job
And the church is neglected
And my family suffers
And I get exhausted and sick
And my wife gets bitter and depressed
And my daughter grows up angry at God?

What will happen –
When I pray with Hannah
And God doesn't answer
And I can't wait
And my daughter shares my fear
And trembles in her own strength
And wonders about God's faithfulness
And His power to intervene
And walks away from the faith?

What if I pray –
When the medical bills come
And the claim is denied
And I get another job
And more ministry opportunities come
And the church comes together
And shares the ministry
And more gets done for Eternity
Than I could have accomplished alone?

What if I trust –
When I pray with Hannah
And God doesn't answer
And I teach her to wait
And she learns steadfastness
And displays perseverance
And the answer comes finally
And God's glory is magnified
And she delights in her God?

If you then, though you are evil, know how to give
good gifts to your children, how much more will
your Father in heaven give the Holy Spirit to those
who ask him!"
(Luke 11:13)

Does the Day Ever End?

Rush, rush, rush! Push, push, push!
> Does the day ever end? Does the work ever get
> finished? Is the job ever done?

Nag, nag, nag! Cajole, cajole, cajole!
> Will the kids ever listen? Will they ever get the
> message? Will they ever get the job
> done without me hounding them to death about it?

How am I going to get everything done?
> What if it's not done well enough?
How can I balance all the responsibilities at home?
> What if something falls through the cracks?

We only have two children, and we're rushing
> all the time; how did my wife's parents ever do it
> with six kids? Are we just too busy today?

Lord, there is no limit to the sources of anxiety in my life!
You know them well.
> We just bought a new house;
>> will we be able to pay for it?
> Our car has 130,000 miles on it;
>> will it break down on the freeway in Cleveland?
> Our daughter is beautiful and popular;
>> have we taught her well enough about boys and
>> how to conduct herself as a Christian and with
>> integrity?

O Lord, you are the Rock that can steady me when I'm
feeling anxious, tossed by the waves.

Yes, there is more going on in my life than I can ever
hope to "control"; yet, you remind me that I don't have to
control everything, that you have everything under
                                        Your control.

Teach me to cast my anxieties upon you,
      and to give you charge over my worries.
Help me to discern that which is worthy of my concern,
      from that which is not.
Help me to learn the difference between
      those things that I can fix, and
      those things that only you can fix.

I trust and believe that you have my life, and the life of
      my family, in your loving and merciful hands.
And throughout all my years,
      you, Lord, have never forsaken me;
You have never failed to be with me,
      to care for me, to love me.

Enable me to go forth
            to live, to serve, to parent, and to pastor
            in that knowledge, and with this confidence:
                  I will put my trust in no other,
                  I will put my trust in you;

Keep me, and those I love, always in the palm of your
hand,
                  all the days of our lives!

*Cast all your anxiety on him because he cares for
you.*
                  (1 Peter 5:7)

I Have Carried This Sadness
Full Term

Sadness has robbed me of my joyful countenance;
a dark foreboding permeates my soul.
Sluggishness is precipitated in my gait;
words do not come easy for me.

The pain of my sadness is childbirth intensified;
my soul is pregnant with melancholy.
My spirit is in the trimester of sorrow;
I have carried this sadness full-term.

Is it this sadness (the holocaust of my soul)
that will disintegrate the freedom of my spirit?

Is it in this dark night of the soul
      that I will find the key
            to unlock the door
                  to the darker night
                      of my spirit?

Am I destined to
      ever live
      my life
      in this
      darkened
      state?

I cry out to you, My God...
My tears soak my pillow at night.
Free me from this sadness,
create in me a clean heart,
and impregnate me with your Joy...

Restore the joy of my salvation, My God.
Let Joybells ring in my soul!

*I am a woman who is deeply troubled. I have not
been drinking wine or beer; I was pouring my soul
to the Lord. Do not take your servant for a wicked
woman; I have been praying here out of my great
anguish and grief.*
(1 Samuel 1:15-16)

Is There *Anyone* in Your House
I Can Trust?

Lord, I feel like I am at war; I can't trust anyone.

People in my own congregation seek to destroy me!
    I feel like hiding!
    Is there anyplace to hide that is safe?

People talk, and others listen.

So many colleagues have lost their livelihood.
    They studied hard,
    got their degrees,
    answered Your call,

                            and have been
                                tossed
                                out.

I feel at times like there is no security in your call.
I am scared that my career will end like theirs.
I am scared that I will have no place to go.

The ironic thing is that you told me
                    it would be this way at times.

I am not as strong as I thought! O God,
give me courage! I am trembling with thoughts of
tomorrow. Where will I go? What will I do?

I know these feelings may not be legit,
however, I am feeling this way,
and I don't know what to do about it.

Is there anyone in your house I can trust?

I have all of this energy, but at times am afraid to lead,
for fear of a will aimed arrow! Words hurt! I get shot
at much of the time. Will you protect me, Lord?

Can I crawl into your strong arms and stay there for
a while? Could you give me peace and shelter?
   I really need you, Lord!

There are those in your house who take no thought
of my family. They are only concerned with power
and control.

If I stay a "yes man," my future may be a little more
secure. Should I live with my tail between my legs?

I fear I will lose integrity in exchange for job
security. Please don't allow that to happen to me,

Lord!
   Make me strong!
   Give me your courage to stand!
   Help me to stand on the principles
     you have given me.
   Don't allow me to be afraid of men,
     of a man.
   Give me courage to take a stand.

Lord, please go before me.
   Please allow me to
     take shelter beneath your wings.
   Please lift me upon your strong wings.
   May I find contentment in knowing that
     You are with me.

I feel safe as you go before me.

Why do I have such a hard time even trusting you?
You have always been faithful to me.
　　　You are so awesome!

I feel like Elijah at times. I want to hide in a cave.
Thank you for being there for me.

Thank you for overpowering those that seek my
demise.

You are so great!
　　　I love you with all my heart!

*The Lord said, "Go out and stand on the mountain
in the presence of the Lord, for the Lord is about to
pass by." Then a great and powerful wind tore the
mountain apart and shattered the rocks before the
Lord, but the Lord was not in the wind. After the
wind there was an earthquake, but the Lord was not
in the earthquake. After the earthquake came a fire,
but the Lord was not in the fire. And after the fire
came a gentle whisper. When Elijah heard it, he
pulled his cloak over his face and went out and
stood at the mount of the cave. Then a voice said to
him, "What are you doing here?"*
　　　　　　　(1 Kings 19:11-13)

I am Sad, Lord

O Lord my God, my heart is heavy.
    My father is taken from me.
    The cruel hand of death has
        snatched him away,
    and my heart is very sad.

No more will I see the twinkle in his eye
    or see the smile upon his face.
No more will I hear his cheerful greeting
    every morning.
No more is he a part of my life.

All I have left are my memories...
                    and I am sad.

But You, O Lord, You are the one who gives joy
back to those who mourn.
    For You have said, *"Blessed are those who
    mourn, for they shall be comforted."*

And You are the Giver and Restorer of life.
    For You have said, *"I am the resurrection
    and the life. Whosoever believes in Me will
    never die."*

My father lived in that hope,
    and I know he is not disappointed.

Therefore, Lord, I too will rejoice and
               put my trust in You.

In the hope of the resurrection,
      will I wait to see my father once again.

I will praise Your holy Name for
      Your love and goodness to Your people.

O give thanks and praise to the Lord,
      for by His grace,
                  I am comforted.

Blessed are those who mourn,
 for they shall be comforted.
                (Matthew 5:4)

Jesus said to her, "I am the resurrection and the
life. He who believes in me will live, even though
he dies. And, whoever lives and believes in me will
never die."
                (John 11:25-26)

Thy Mystery of
Unanswered Questions

Where, O God, where are You?
        You hide from me,
There is no one to answer.

Life goes on;
        with it is the mystery of
        unanswered questions.

You tell us you are love,
        but love remains quiet.
You tell us to trust; it is so hard.

Brother dies,
        and we know not why.
Evil laughs at good;
        You seem to be powerless.

I turn to myself and I have no power, no voice.
I turn to You because there is no other.

In Your mystery
        You hold me and care for me with a
                love I do not understand.
                A mystery.

I do not concern myself with great matters,
 or things too wonderful for me.
                        (Psalm 131:1b)

A Wolf has Infiltrated the Flock

Lord, I'm looking for you. I remember the past
when it seemed that everywhere I turned, there you
were!

Where have you gone?

So often, I found you in the old hymns: *Amazing
Grace! There is a Balm in Gilead!* I found you in
the *Little Church in the Wildwood!* Yet, now you
seem conspicuously absent.

Where have you gone?

In days gone by, I found you in my work. I was
productive. I knew where I was going. My
accomplishments were many, and people were
proud to call me pastor. I was a gentle shepherd –
they said, "Just like Jesus." Now, the gentle
shepherd doesn't seem so gentle to some. A wolf
has infiltrated the flock, but the flock only sees his
sheep's clothing.

Where are you, Lord?

I saw you in the eyes of the flock.
There was encouragement in their bleating.
Their hearts were filled hope.
Like sheep, they trusted the gentle shepherd.
They trusted me.
Now questions abound.
Insecurity is in their eyes.

Their insecure bleating, their worried question
grow louder; so loud that I can barely hear your
voice over the din.

Where are you, Lord?

I remember the times that my work was a great joy.
Now the primary task in my work is worry. I see
the question in the eyes of your people, "Is pastor
leading us to destruction, or toward greener pastures
and the way that leads to eternal life?" Their hearts
cry out as my heart, "Where are you, Lord?'

Where have you gone?"

At times like these I have retreated into solitude
to observe the beauty of nature.
Then, I could almost see your hand
as it moved across creation.
Recently, creation was coated with
the pure beauty of new fallen snow.
It was like my countenance in past times when
you felt so near –
pure, tranquil and beautiful.

My life was like the earth covered by new fallen
snow. It was beautiful. Now, my countenance has
fallen. The beauty is gone as the purity of the new
fallen snow melts away, turning the earth to a sea of
mud.

Lord, where have you gone?

Worry and the knot in my stomach are
my closest companions.

84

My mind turns the questions
      over and over like a stone:
      What if the people refuse to follow?
      What, if the people rebel?
      What if I am wrong?
            What if?
            What if?
            What if?
            What if?
                   Lord, where have you gone?

I need direction.
      I need assurance.
            I need the stability of
            your presence and
            your love.

I'll keep looking for you, Lord,
                 but will you be found?

Remember your promise, that I seek and find you
if I search for you with my whole heart.

*"For I know the plans I have for you," declares the
Lord, "plans to prosper you and not to harm you,
plans to give you hope and a future. Then you will
call upon me and come and pray to me, and I will
listen to you. You will seek me and find me when
you seek me with your heart.*
                    (Jeremiah 29:11-13)

A Parent Who Does Not Love

As for me, I can give God praise,
      for surely the Lord has never forsaken me.

But Lord,
      why have you given me a parent
      who does not love?

Why, Lord, have you taken a parent
      who did love?

Forsaken on both accounts,
      on you, Lord, I must totally depend.

But why Lord?

Can a mother forget the baby at her breast
 and have no compassion on the child she has
 borne?
Though she may forget,
 I will not forget you!
I have engraved you on the palms of my hands;
 your walls are ever before me.
               (Isaiah 49:15-16)

I Find Comfort in Him

Do not be overcome with anxiety,
    even when things look hopeless.
God is in control and he will not
    let you fall or get in over your head.

How easy it is to imagine the worst
    and fret away the time with worry.
Did not the Father stand beside all
    His children in calamity and struggle?

He made us and all we see around us; He is faithful.
He never fails to be present in our time of need.

I am encouraged to know that
    He is always near.
His faithfulness is present, even
    for those who do not love Him.

I find comfort in Him no matter
    what seems to bother me.
When I turn to Him, I am
    never disappointed.

Here is a trustworthy saying:
    If we died with him,
      we will also live with him;
    if we endure;
      we will also reign with him.
    If we disown him,
      he will also disown us;
    if we are faithless,
      he will remain faithful,
      for he cannot disown himself.
            (2 Timothy 2:11-13)

When the Pastor's
Spouse Prays

My Daddy

O God,

        You are awesome

You have forgiven me and loved me
in spite of my
        faults,
        shortcomings,
        and sins.

You continue to give me
        grace,
        mercy,
        and peace.

I praise you forever and ever!
You are
        my comfort,
        my strength,
        and my Daddy.

*For you did not receive a spirit that makes you a
slave again to fear, but you received the Spirit of
sonship. And by him we cry, "Abba, Father." The
Spirit himself testifies with our spirit that we are
God's children.*
        (Romans 8:15-16)

I Can Live for You

Oh God, You are the best thing
       that has ever happened to me.

I cannot count the times
       You've been there without me asking
       or sometimes even begin aware!

In the times I am low and feeling alone,
       You're there, even when
       I blame You for being far away.

Although I blame You, You are blameless,
       for I am the one who has moved, not You!

You continue to be my strength,
       my source of peace, and my comforter.

I praise You for choosing me to be Your daughter,
       Your princess,
       Your Kingdom child.

Thank You for taking the blame for me
       so I can live for You.
       Help me to do just that!
Amen!
Your daughter, princess, and Kingdom child

As the Father has loved me, so have I loved you.
Now remain in my love.
             (John 15:9)

Lord, I have Many Masks

Dear Lord, right now You know,
    as You always have,
        who I am and
        why I am and
        what I am.

I have so many masks
That I've lost all sense of myself.

I sometimes wonder
      if I am of any use to anyone,
      let alone to myself
             or to You.

I want to surrender all of this to You so I can just
      be someone who is real and
      has an identity.

Most of all,
   I want to be
      someone who my husband will respect;
   I want to be
      the best possible helpmate for him,

But then again I wonder if this is possible
      even with You as my guide,

…only because I feel
      I'm not worth the
         trouble or
         time.

But the struggles will be gone
when, soon, my life will be gone.

I wish I were young again
with the wisdom of my age
and the courage of Your love
so my life would not be a total waste.

I wish I'd never again feel
the pain or rejection,
loneliness, or
wanting to be loved
and accepted.

I wish my husband could accept me
as he does others.

I really don't want to give up.
I want to be fulfilled and whole,
and of service to You.

With Your help, I will survive.

Thank you for listening to me.

Find rest, O my soul, in God alone;
My hope comes from him.
(Psalm 62:5)

I'm so Angry at You

Pat is dying, Lord,
      and I feel like You don't give a hoot
      how that is affecting any of us–
Let alone her family –
      or will affect us;
      if, in fact, You do not seem
      to be providing the miracle
      we're all praying for.

I'm so upset with You
      that it has left me unable to pray
      without screaming at You.
I'm so angry at You.

You are allowing Pat to die –
Pat, the one who came to know You late,
      compared to me –
But who is such an example to me of
      how to live for You –
      uncluttered by past and
                  baggage.

What blessing and encouragement she is to
      all who know her –
Even now as You are letting her die.

Lord, she has so much life and godliness;
      she will bring honor to Your name,
      and I don't want You to let her die.

Well, there, I've said it,
            and it's pretty much total selfishness
                    on my part.

She loves You and, yes, Lord, I do love You –
and I'm asking that her example –
even in death –
will continue to inspire me.

Thank you for accepting this from me.

Hear my prayer, O Lord;
  Let my cry for help come to you.
Do not hide your face from me
  When I am in distress.
                            (Psalm 102:1-2)

Protect My Husband Lord!

God,
>   do You know what is going on in my life?

Your children are hurting one of their own,
>   accusing without knowledge,
>   judging by past experience,
>   not asking for Your guidance.
>   Giving orders from mortal eyes.

I praise You from the depths of my heart
for the strength and love You give me.

I stand firm in Your Presence
knowing You guide my steps.

Do not fret because of evil men
* Or be envious of those who do wrong;*
For like the grass they will soon wither,
* Like green plants they will soon die away.*
*   (Psalm 37:1-2)*

I Don't Feel Loved

O God, You are a good God
and You have been with me in the darkness,
holding me in the palm of Your hand.

You continue to keep loving me
even when I don't feel loved.
Help me to never rely on my feelings.

I praise You for never leaving me
or forsaking me in my time of need.

Teach me Your ways
and show me a way to balance my life
that would bring You praise,
                glory,
                and honor.

Thank you for Your gift of life today.

Teach me to do your will,
* for you are my God;*
may your good Spirit
* lead me on level ground.*
*   (Psalm 143:10)*

You Bless Us

Oh, God,
> You are a wonder-working,
> awesome God.

You bring miracles of joy
when we don't deserve anything.

You bless us
beyond our wildest dreams.

You have brought us
an amazing, beautiful angel boy
who fills our hearts with sunshine and laughter.

You continue to amaze me
as You have brought the possibility
of another baby blessing into our lives.

Please, Lord,
> I pray that this will be Your will
> > and Your desire.
I know, Lord, that You want to give us
> the desires of our hearts,
> and You know that another child
> is what we truly want.

Please help me to be content
            with whatever You want
            and to rest in Your comfort,
                        concern,
                        and love.

I praise You for the provision
            and the many blessings
            that You have heaped upon us.

Your grace and provision
            are a constant source
            of amazement to me!

My soul praises the Lord
  and my spirit rejoices in God my savior,
for he has been mindful of the humble state of his
servant.
                (Luke 1:46-48a)

100

The Sandberg Leadership Center
on the Campus of Ashland Theological Seminary

Don't do what the world needs
Do what keeps you alive;
For what the world needs
Is you, alive!
Howard Thurman

The Sandberg Leadership Center is located on the Campus of Ashland Theological Seminary. From the heart of northeast Ohio, the center serves the growing need for quality leadership training throughout the United States.

Leadership is at a time of transition. The "hero-leader" of the past is no longer adequate for the relational world of the new century. Before there can be real change in our institutions, there must be change in our understanding and practice of leadership.

OUR MISSION

We are a center of transformational learning, committed to the spiritual and character formation of servant leaders who will make a difference in business, government, church, and society.

We practice transformational learning...

- Transformational learning produces reflective leaders of integrity, courage, and wisdom.

We commit to spiritual and character formation...

- Leaders express clear, personal core values in competencies consistent with good leadership.

We believe servant leaders make a difference...

- Leadership is the ability to get things done. Servant leadership accomplishes tasks by investing in people.

We serve leaders in business, government, church, and society.

- The Center will focus on developing leadership in business, government, church, and society.

OUR VALUES

The Leadership Center is committed to a biblical understanding of life, education, and ministry:

- We value **servant leadership** as the biblical model.

- We value **spiritual formation** that results in life renewed and the recovery of identity in Christ.

- We value **self-understanding** and **discovery**.

- We value **team building** and shared responsibility within the organization.

- We value the vision of the leader as a **change agent** in the organization and society.

- We value Christian **witness** and **mission**.

- We value **academic excellence**.

- We value the **redemption, personal healing,** and **equipping** of each participant.

- We value an attitude of **stewardship** and a careful **discernment of the culture.**

SEEING THE FUTURE, NOW

The decades of changing culture has shaken the foundations of business, government and the church. The older ways of management treat the church, business, and government as machines. The new paradigm, formed through servant leadership, views organization in personal images of teams, networks, and partners or in biblical images of "family," "body," and "living stones."

Transition is traumatic. There are loud voices from the "not too distant past" calling for structures that stifle creativity and diminish the energy of relationships. Yet, there is a still voice from the "not too distant future" that longs for leadership. But, it is not necessarily a cry for more leaders, or better leaders, but a cry for a different kind of leader: one who is empowered by the synergy of servant leadership and spiritual formation in renewing the organization on a True Foundation.

Such a leader is competent in two skills:

- **The forming of self as servant leader**.
- **The forming of the organization as servant people**.

This leader is equipped to move the organization toward a system of relationship and empowerment. It is our purpose at The Leadership Center to model the new paradigm as we provide transformational learning for Christian leaders in business, government and the church.

CONTACT US

If we can serve you in leadership training; if you would like information on programs available for you and your organization; or if you would like to know how you can participate in the development of The Leadership Center, contact us at:

**The Sandberg Leadership Center
910 Center Street
Ashland, Ohio   44805**

Email: LeadOn@ashland.edu

1-419-289-5323(LEAD)

Richard L. Parrott, Ph.D.
Executive Director

Richard Leslie Parrott, Executive Director
The Sandberg Leadership Center
Of Ashland Theological Seminary

Dr. Parrott is the Executive Director of The Sandberg Leadership Center in Ashland, Ohio. The Center is dedicated to Transformational Leadership in business, government and the church. Dr. Parrott has worked collaboratively with leadership centers at Yale Divinity School, Claremont School of Theology, and the Gordon-Conwell School of Theology.

Richard Leslie Parrott is also the Director of the Doctor of Ministry Program at Ashland Theological Seminary in Ashland, Ohio. Dr. Parrott works with over one hundred pastors from twenty-five denominations and many world areas. His teaching in the doctoral program includes course work in Transformational Leadership including: *"Political Reality and Spiritual Leadership," "Organizing for Spiritual Renewal,"* and *"Leading Profound Change."*

He was educated at Eastern Nazarene College (B.A.), University of Missouri (M.A. in Psychology), Nazarene Theological Seminary (M.Div.), and received his Ph.D. from Oregon State University in Education Administration. He has received further education from the Executive School of University of Michigan in Ann Arbor, Michigan.

Dr. Parrott has guided both boards and individuals in pursuit of Leadership Excellence at the Strategic Leadership Conference in Seattle, Washington, the Ohio State Board of Pharmacy, the State of Ohio Convention for Chamber of Commerce, Values-Based Impact for Non-Profits in San Francisco, California, and the Lilly Leadership Grant program on Non-Profit Organizations at Yale University.
Dr. Parrott is a resident of Ashland, Ohio where he is an active participant in the community. He is on the Board of the Chamber of Commerce and Leadership Ashland.

Dr. Parrott speaks extensively. His duties include faculty participation in Church Planting Seminars and Church Health and Renewal Seminars. He is a frequent speaker for conferences, seminars, and special events.